Three-Dimensional Team Building:

Building Teams to Succeed in Every Aspect of the Game

First Printing: 2019

ISBN 978-0-578-60273-8

Chapter 1: This is a Team Game

Growing up, the Payne household was centered around sports. I didn't identify the seasons as "Summer, Fall, Winter, and Spring", but as "Football, Basketball, and Baseball." We talked about sports, read about sports, played sports and watched sports. If there was a ball involved, we were into it. Actually, I need to make an adjustment to those statements. We were into TEAM sports. I knew people who played golf and tennis but those weren't "real" sports to me because they were played by individuals. Upon further review, I see the faultiness of my logic in regards to the definition of a "sport," but I can also clearly see why football, baseball and basketball were so attractive to me. Those games were not just about winning. They were about winning TOGETHER. To be successful, disparate individuals had to function as an integrated unit. Yes, each team had big stars but those stars were surrounded by role players and whether they were all-stars or no-stars, they shared a common uniform and a common goal that required each of them to play their part so the ultimate goal could be achieved. Obviously, the impact of teams when it comes to being successful goes way beyond the basketball court, football field or baseball diamond. Maybe it's just my skewed perspective but the creation of teams and the constant call for collaboration seems to have expanded into every aspect of society, from the classroom to the board room and beyond. And quite frankly, as budgets get smaller within and between organizations, the necessity of putting groups together to accomplish larger goals is only going to grow. Therefore, the question isn't whether or not we will have and be a part of teams, but how do we build teams that are designed for success.

The truth is we've been exposed to the concept of teams since our earliest days of elementary school. I know you remember standing on the basketball court just hoping to be picked by someone to be a part of the team. Or how about the agony of the teacher not only assigning a group project, but choosing those you would work with as well? Then again, maybe it was worse when the teacher let us pick our own partner for the project. Regardless of the environment, teams were a part of our formative years. And while these experiences probably didn't impact the state of world politics for decades to come, I believe those opportunities deeply affected how we form, join, and work within teams today. In fact, some of us don't consider ourselves team-players as we are haunted by memories of partners who didn't do any work on that project in 8th grade science. Because we didn't have positive experiences with teams in the past, we do everything we can to avoid being joined to a team in our current affairs. Unfortunately, with the rise of teaming agreements and cooperative efforts, this "anti-team" philosophy will ultimately be detrimental to our personal success and ironically, to the success of the teams forming around us.

Similar to my desire to write a book on followership, a book on team-building seemed appropriate because even though we've been building, joining, and operating in teams all our lives, I'm not sure too many of us have actually considered how we go about putting teams together and signing up to join those teams to ensure success on all fronts. We do what we've always done and then sadly, we get what we've always gotten. Our teams tend to be good at one thing and not-so-good at others. That's why the subtitle of the book is "Building Teams to Succeed in Every Aspect of the Game." Just like *Three-Dimensional Leadership* and *Three-Dimensional Followership*, the aspects of this game involve the task, the team and the individuals involved. Maybe it's just me, but until I started working on this book, I never considered all three of these areas when I was making and participating in teams. Some teams are built for specific tasks and must accomplish that task to be successful. Therefore, anyone building or joining a team must do so with the END in mind. However, when a team is able to accomplish the END of a task but the members that make up that team don't work well together, the team is ultimately going to suffer. I mean, how many amazing collections of athletes have we seen win a lot of games, and maybe even championships, but the individual players were labelled as being bad teammates? There was a responsibility expected of the players beyond making shots and winning games. Each member of the team was expected to be beneficial to the other members of that team. When they weren't, the team suffered and never achieved their full potential. Therefore, a major consideration for the team is the BLEND of the team. How do the individual team members impact the overall structure and effectiveness of the team? Finally, a well-built team will not only take care of the task and work well together, but will have processes and procedures in place to take care of the individual team members. While asking the "what's in it for me?" question is often frowned upon, it is a very important question because we need to know if being a part of this team will help us move forward in life. On the other side, when we build teams, because there are so many out there, those of us responsible for making decisions must determine why someone should join our team. What distinguishes our team from the myriad of other teams out there? Both those forming teams and those joining teams need to consider the TEND of the team. How does the team take care of the team members? A team that treats people like commodities to be used and thrown away at a moment's notice will never achieve true success.

Before I continue, I should probably clarify what I mean by "team." The second definition of "team" from Dictionary.com defines a team as "a number of persons associated in some joint action."[1] I feel that definition is necessary because too often people think of teams as only those who participate in an athletic event. However, for the purpose of this book, "team" will take on a broader meaning

---

[1] https://www.dictionary.com/browse/team, accessed 28 May 2019.

of a group of two or more individuals organized to work together. Throughout the book I will use other words for "team" such as "organization," "partnership," and "group" to help us see the reach of the "team" definition.

Team-building is the natural culmination point of this series of *Three-Dimensional* books. After all, the terms "leader" and "follower" imply the forming a team, being part of a team or joining a team. Therefore, when you are a leader and you are tasked to put together a team, how do you do that? When you are a follower, and you have a choice to join a team, how do you decide if that team is right for you? My desire is that this book will tie together the other two books as we move forward to not only being successful as individuals but also successful within environments that require partnership and team play. Life is a team game and the better we play, the better everyone else will be.

Taking a 3-D Look at Your Team

1. Are you a team player?

2. How do you define a team?

3. What were the traits of the best team you were ever part of?

4. What were the traits of the worst team you were ever part of?

5. For the worst team you were ever apart of, would it have been possible to bring that team together?

Chapter 2: Build the Team for the END of the Task
Begin with the end in mind.
-- Stephen Covey

On those rare weekends when there is nothing formal on the schedule for the Payne family, my wife and I will plan to just get in the car and go. Maybe we'll have breakfast or visit an estate sale or go give platelets. The bottom line to those days is we are going to do things we consider fun, and do them together. However, because I'm a planner, this kind of spontaneity messes with my inner sensibilities so I have to have some sort of plan. So while Linda is just ready to jump in the car, I am walking around asking one basic question, "What's the END of the day?" You see, before I start something, I want to know where we are going. Knowing where we are going will help me make the necessary decisions about which way to go, what must be done and what can wait, and how long do we plan on being at each location. I will accept deviations from the plan but I will not accept not starting with a plan. Now this may sound obvious to a lot of people but I'm not wholly convinced we consider the END when we are putting teams together.

Remember the definition of "team" we identified in the previous chapter mentioned a group associated for "joint action." And the action is certainly important but what is the END of the action. If we're working on a class project, are we looking for an "A" or do we just want to pass? On the football field, is the team focused on having a winning season, making the playoffs or winning the championship? I've told anyone who will listen that if we are keeping score, winning matters. If we just want to play Spades by dealing the cards, playing the hand, and then shuffling the cards without writing down the number of books each team took, then I'm fine. The END is simply to just have fun. However, if someone pulls out a piece of paper and a pen and writes names on the paper, in my mind, the END is no longer to just "have fun," but to win. Now because Spades is a team game, my partner and I need to agree on the END so we can effectively work together. While we could still win the game, our disagreement on the END of the game would probably result in some frustration as the manner in which we move to achieve our individual ENDS collide with one another.

An understanding of the END of the task is essential to how the team is formed. While the old saying says, "the END justifies the means," when it comes to team building, "the END of the task provides the means for building the team." The ones charged with putting teams together must begin not with the people who are available but with what is the END of the task the team is being formed to accomplish. However, I would be remiss if I didn't mention the fact that a person looking to join a particular team must consider the END of that team as well. As I've mentioned several times before, I'm a hyper-competitive guy so if the team I'm looking at joining just "wants to have fun" then that's probably not the team for me. It's not that they are bad people or that their organization is misguided. It's simply a matter of the END of the team not matching with my personal desires. I know we could eliminate a lot of problems with team building if people, team builders and team joiners, would consider the END of the task in the earliest stages of forming the group. In the environment of three-dimensional team building, all those involved with the team must understand the END of the task; which for our purposes means knowing the **E**ffort required for the task, the **N**ature of the task, and the **D**uration of the task. With a good understanding of these qualities of the task, a team can be put together to succeed.

The achievements of an organization are the results of the combined effort of each individual.

-- Vince Lombardi

Ever since I started pastoring I've had a love-hate relationship with the King James Version of the bible. For those who don't know, the King James Version, or KJV, is written in Old 17th century English. To show you the difference, one of my favorite verses is found in the book of Joshua, chapter 1, verse 7. In the KJV, this verse reads, "Only be thou strong and very courageous, that thou mayest observe to do according to all the law, which Moses my servant commanded thee: turn not from it to the right hand or to the left, that thou mayest prosper withersoever thou goest." Now I don't know about you, but I can't remember the last time I used the words "thou", "mayest", and

9

"whithersoever" in an everyday conversation. Now the New King James Version, or NKJV, takes the Old English of the KJV and makes it more readable for a contemporary audience and renders the aforementioned verse as, "Only be strong and very courageous, that you may observe to do according to all the law which Moses My servant commanded you; do not turn from it to the right hand or to the left, that you may prosper wherever you go." At this point many of us would say, "Why didn't you just say that in the first place?"

I bring this up because most Christians learned to read the bible in the KJV and we've developed an aptitude to decipher the archaic language that's become second nature for us. The EFFORT required for us to understand and operate is minimal. This is a good thing until we bring others to the team. Since reading the KJV requires little EFFORT for us, we assume everyone else we invite to join us can manage the "thees," "thous," and "haths" with the same dexterity that we do. However, if you've ever been in a church and seen a 9-year old trying to read the scripture for the day in the KJV, you can clearly see there's a different level of EFFORT for this child. I cringe because I know this poor child has no idea what she is reading and she's being turned off from the team and enjoying the greatest book ever written since it appears to be printed in a foreign language. I cringe even more when parents and other church leaders force this version on their children saying, "if you're going to be on this 'church team,' you are going to have to use this version of the bible."

Because we failed to understand the EFFORT required for the task for all parties involved, we run the risk of running people away from the group we are trying to form.

The EFFORT is the level of difficulty of the task or the individual tasks that team members will be asked to perform to support completion of the overall task. Is the task fit for a beginner without much experience or technical aptitude? Is the job more appropriate for someone with some familiarity with the task? Is this the type of job that calls for an intermediate or advanced worker? And as mentioned with the KJV example, a task that doesn't demand much EFFORT for one person may require much more EFFORT for another. Failure to acknowledge the different levels of difficulty necessary could put the team in danger of having members who feel overqualified for the task at hand and having other members who don't have the tools necessary to get the job done. Many of us have been in positions where the level of EFFORT demanded of us was much less than our capability and even though the job was simple, we didn't do it with the highest level of our ability because we were unfulfilled. In my view, this is an issue caused by carelessness to the END by both the team builder and the team member. The team builder failed to set realistic expectations of the EFFORT vital to finishing the task while the team member failed to be a "team player" and do the job they were assigned to the best of their ability, even if the EFFORT was beneath their skills and talents.

At the end of every semester when I was an ROTC instructor at North Carolina A&T State University, I taught a class on the officer's oath of office. I saved this lesson for the very last class before the students were going to receive their commissions as second lieutenants. In the midst of the oath, those to be commissioned repeat the phrase, *"I will well and faithfully discharge the duties of the office I am about to enter."* During the class I asked each student what the duties were of the office they were about to enter. They always repeated back to me their career fields. *"I am going to fly."* *"I am going to handle finances."* *"I'm going to do intelligence work."* They were proud of their answers because those answers for the most part represented what they wanted to do. I hated to bust their bubbles (actually I didn't. I rather enjoyed it.), but their answers were shortsighted because they weren't entering the service as pilots, intelligence officers, finance officers, cops, or missileers. They were entering the service as second lieutenants which meant their actual duties were going to be assigned by those that outranked them. So while they might indeed fly and manage base finances, they were also going to be tasked to be snack officers or be responsible for emptying the trash on Fridays. Now, the level of EFFORT between flying a B-52 and picking up junk food from the grocery store are vastly different. However, both are responsibilities of being a part of the team and deserve the best EFFORT of the individual involved. As the officer ultimately responsible placing these young men and women on the Air Force team, I had to make sure these new team members understood that the EFFORT necessary to make the Air Force work may at times be below their college educations and their personal sensibilities. Our teams will be woefully ineffective if leaders and followers alike don't account for the EFFORT necessary for the task. Or to put it in terms those who love the KJV will understand, "If thou won't considereth fully and giveth all that thou hast to the EFFORT of the task thou hast been given, then thou and all those thou hast teamed with shall fail to the uttermost."

If a man cannot do brain work without stimulants of any kind, he had better turn to hand work. It is an indication on Nature's part that she did not mean him to be a head worker.
-- Thomas Huxley

My dad loved working in the yard. It was like he worked all week just so he could buy flowers, fertilizer, and lawn equipment to spend all day Saturday in the yard. And of course, what my father loved, he expected me to love as well. Truth be told, he didn't care if I loved working in the yard. He just expected me to join him and do the work. And because I still have all my teeth, you know that I joined him out in the yard without complaint. It's been over 30 years since those days and quite often when I shake my father's hand, he comments on how soft my hands are. While he means that comment as a playful jab, I take it as a badge of honor because I've spent all the years since living in my father's house avoiding anything that looks like yard work. In fact, you could say I work all week to pay someone else to spend time in my yard. It's not that I can't do the work. I certainly can. However, I just don't want to. The NATURE of yard work isn't what I want to do so I've spent a lot of time dodging it, and tasks like it, as much as possible.

While this makes me sound weak and less manly to many, I know I'm not alone. The NATURE of a task is the deciding factor for many people applying for a job or accepting an assignment. Therefore, team builders must consider the task's NATURE if they are going to put a successful team together. The NATURE of the task is the "how" of the task that consists of the type of work required to complete the task. Is the task hands-on or mental? Will the task be performed indoors or outdoors? Will those charged to complete the task need some ability with tools or computers? The answers to these questions, and those like them, are imperative when forming an organization to get the job done. If you are putting together a lawn maintenance business, while I am definitely capable of cutting grass and trimming hedges, I'm not the guy you want because the NATURE of the work is contrary to who I am and what I want to do.

Because as the adage says, "there's more than one way to skin a cat," the NATURE of the task is often dependent on how the organizer plans to attack the task. Just because someone can do a task, they may not be able to accomplish the task in the manner in which the leader decided was appropriate. I ran into this "NATURE" problem when I was in graduate school. In an attempt to "give back" to the community, I volunteered to serve as a math tutor for high school students. Eventually I received a call that a couple of twin girls needed help with their 12th grade calculus class. Admittedly it had been a while since I had done calculus but I felt up for the challenge. When I showed up at the house, the girls and I sat down at the dining room table and they explained they were having issues understanding how to do integration problems. (For those who have no idea what an integration problem is, feel free to call your favorite math nerd and have him or her explain it. It'll be good bonding time for the two of you.) After the explanation, I pulled out a piece of paper and a pencil and started to write out the first problem. As I was beginning to diagram the problem, one of the girls stopped me and said, "We don't want you to show us how to do the problems on there (pointing to the paper), we need you to show us on this (holding up a calculator). Well, I went to college shortly after the invention of the calculator watch so when I was doing this kind of math, calculators did not exist that could do this type of problem. The calculator we used was a stubby pencil, lots of paper, and a human brain. What both the girls and I realized that while finding someone to help with the task of learning how to do integration problems is important, it's even more important to consider the NATURE of the task when selecting that someone. The ladies found someone, but not the right someone and our

15

team was completely ineffective because I couldn't complete the task how they wanted it done.

We have seen an incredible amount of change in the manner in which we can complete tasks. Heck, just a few years ago we had to actually get up off the couch to turn the channel on the TV and now certain cable providers allow you to change the channel with your voice. The NATURE of work is changing nearly every day and if team builders don't maintain a clear understanding of how the task in front of them needs to be addressed, they run the risk of adding people to the team who are incapable getting the job done. The desire to complete the task is great, but if the desire isn't accompanied by the ability to complete the task in the prescribed way, then failure is the only option. Just ask the guy trying to use a #2 pencil in a calculator world.

In short, you can't let the deadline define the mission. The mission has to define the duration.

-- Richard Holbrooke

Since I have been ordained as a minister, I have had the pleasure of performing marriages in at least 10 different states. The first thing I do when asked to perform a wedding in a new place is check out the laws for marriage in that state. Many people are shocked to know there are some very diverse rules on how to and who can perform weddings across the country. One of the more interesting laws about marriage is in the state of Louisiana. In the Pelican State, couples can either sign up for a "standard" marriage or a "covenant" marriage. A covenant marriage is a marriage where a couple takes additional steps to affirm their commitment that marriage is a lifelong relationship. Therefore, the difference between a standard marriage and covenant marriage is the DURATION. While those engaging in a standard marriage may make a public statement during their ceremony that they will stay together until "death do them part," a couple entering a covenant marriage actually signs a statement of intent filed in the public record that,

> "We do solemnly declare that marriage is a covenant between a man and a woman who agree to live together as husband and wife for so long as they both may live. We have chosen each other carefully and disclosed to one another everything which could adversely affect the decision to enter into this marriage. We have received premarital counseling on the nature, purposes, and responsibilities of marriage. We have read the Covenant Marriage Act, and we understand that a Covenant Marriage is for life. If we experience marital difficulties, we commit ourselves to take all reasonable efforts to preserve our marriage, including marital counseling."

While simply signing this statement doesn't guarantee that the task of being married will last the DURATION of a lifetime, it does highlight the fact that the two people forming this team have determined that they will be a part of this team for as long as it takes. This commitment to DURATION is an often overlooked element of the team building process because most people just assume the teams they join or form will be there for as long as they need to the team to be there.

However, the lifespan of the team is heavily dependent on the DURATION of the task. Too often people assume the group they join will be together forever when the END of the group was in actuality to complete a task in a set time and then disband.

The group formed to complete project in a 7th grade History class has a very different DURATION than the cohort formed in the first year of nursing school. Why is this important? The DURATION matters because if a team is only supposed to be together for a short period of time, then team builders or joiners might make different decisions on how the team is put together. Back to the group project in history class…if I'm weak in history and there's a chance to team with the smartest guy in class to complete the project, I will probably team with him even if I don't like him as long as the DURATION is short enough. Truthfully, I've practiced this more times than I should probably mention when determining what teams, I will or will not join. After I've considered the task before the team, I take a good look at the team members and make a calculated decision if I can put up with those people for the allotted amount of time to complete the task. Don't make that face. You've done it too. Think about your family vacation…the family wanted to go on a summer vacation as a big group. You were forming a team to accomplish the task of enjoying some time together. However, in the forming of the team, you realized that your sister-in-law and her family will be part of this team. During the deliberation process, you don't turn your attention to what the team will be doing but for how long you will be doing it. All of a sudden, DURATION matters in your determination of whether or not you will be a part of this team on this particular task. Three days at Disney is possible, but 14 days on a cruise is out of the question. Why? Because you didn't want to commit to the task of a 14-day trip. The DURATION was too long.

For a task to be successful, every team member must be committed to being on board for the DURATION of the task. There's nothing worse than being part of a team and all of a sudden someone decides the task is taking too long and they drop out. Because they were valued members of the unit, their dropping out caused a disruption in the progress of the team and put success in jeopardy, if not eliminating the possibility of success outright. Team builders can't afford to put together teams with people who aren't planning on being there until the task is complete. Similarly, team joiners shouldn't attach themselves to organizations if they don't plan on sticking around until the work is finished. And in our world today, commitment to long term goals and projects is waning so all parties need to take a serious look at the DURATION of the task the team is assigned before moving forward. Otherwise, you could be a "covenant" team standing alone at the altar when your "standard" team member decides the DURATION was too long.

Taking a 3-D Look at Your Team

1. What is the END your team is working towards?

2. How would you define the EFFORT required to be on your team?

3. What is the NATURE of the tasks members of your team need to accomplish?

4. Are you and your team committed to the DURATION of the task?

Chapter 3: Build the Team for the BLEND of the Team

I think if you look at, for instance, what the Seahawks - what we did winning the Super Bowl, that was with a very young team. So you have to blend the experience with young players and develop those as well.

-- Paul Allen

This might not be the most politically correct statement to make but the greatest stand-up routine of all time is "Bill Cosby Himself." In my days as a young aspiring comedian I actually memorized the entire routine because it was the funniest thing I had ever seen. There were so many great moments in that show that it's hard to narrow it down to one favorite. Near the top of the list is when Bill is telling the story of having to prepare breakfast for his kids. For those uninitiated, Bill tells the story of his wife being sick and him going downstairs to fix the kids breakfast. In the decision making process for what to make for breakfast, the kids ask their father for chocolate cake. He deduces because the cake contains milk and eggs which are breakfast type foods, chocolate cake is the perfect solution to the great breakfast conundrum. But there's another problem. What should he give the kids to drink with their chocolate cake? His answer…grapefruit juice. At that point, the crowd groans and we all know why. Even though orange juice is the quintessential breakfast drink, drinking it with chocolate cake is a pretty disgusting thought. While the combination of orange juice and chocolate cake makes for a great team in a joke, the image points out that two things that might be great

21

separately don't work well together in the real world if they don't BLEND together. Team builders can't just consider the qualities of the individual parts of the team but have to analyze the BLEND of the team to determine if they are building a team that can actually work well together.

My wife is an amazing cook which is a blessing and a curse. It's a blessing because I love to eat so we are a match made in the kitchen. Her culinary gift is a curse because she gets bored cooking the same old things which means she likes to experiment and bring new foods to our dining room table. What's the problem with that you ask? The problem is that I have a very, very small food box. I like what I like and I could eat those items over and over again. I don't really have a desire to eat anything new and different. Therefore, when I go into the kitchen and watch her cook, I have a lot of questions about what she's doing and why she's adding certain items. Those conversations go like this:

Me: *"Why are you putting that in there?"*

Her: *"Don't worry. You won't even be able to taste it."*

Me: *"Well, if I can't taste it, why are you putting it in?"*

The rationale for my complaint is that if the ingredient isn't going to add anything to the flavor of the dish, then it shouldn't be included in the recipe. The way I feel about ingredients in my wife's dishes is the same attitude I see as required when putting a successful team together. If the traits a person brings to the team aren't going to make the team better, why are we adding that person to the team? Whenever I've been in a position to build a team, I've told my leadership that I generally abide by one simple rule… "I will go short before I go stupid." While this statement might sound harsh, it attests to my desire to have the right BLEND of folks on the team and my refusal to just add someone so we reach a magic number to fill all the desks in the office.

Many of us recognize that team dynamics are very fragile and even if we can all agree on the END of the task, there's something wrong if we have constant infighting within the team because the BLEND is wrong. What is the perfect BLEND you ask? That's a great question and in this era of diversity and inclusion, it would seem to mean that the group photo covers all the shades of the ethnic rainbow. However, that's a very shallow view of team dynamics and doesn't necessarily consider the elements that will make sure each team member is good for the health of the team and the team's ability to complete the assigned task. Determining this perfect BLEND of team members is why leaders get the corner office and followers must take their time deciding if a specific team is right for them. For our purposes, identifying that ideal BLEND for the team requires an understanding of what each individual brings to the team in terms of **B**ackground, **L**atency, **E**xperience, **N**etwork, and **D**isposition. Leaders and followers who don't think about the BLEND of the team might as well be putting the proverbial chocolate cake with a big glass of grapefruit juice…and we know nobody is going to like that.

> *Talent and effort, combined with our various backgrounds and life experiences, has always been the lifeblood of our singular American genius.*
>
> *-- Michelle Obama*

My wife has worked for a company handling human resources and hiring for the last few years. Unfortunately, the organization has a pretty high turnover rate which means the team composition is regularly changing and she's got to make sure those applying for positions to join the company will fit within the organization. To do this, not only does the company do a personal interview, but they also do a criminal BACKGROUND check. While the interview allows the supervisors and maybe some coworkers to get a feel for who the person is, the BACKGROUND check is designed to reveal if there is something in a person's past that may make them unfit to be a member of this organization. Unfortunately, like beauty, what makes a person "unfit" is in the eye of the beholder. Nevertheless, a review of a person's BACKGROUND has to be part of the process of team building.

I will offer the caveat that in this information-saturated age we currently live in, those responsible for putting teams together must be careful in the judgements drawn from a person's BACKGROUND. BACKGROUND reviews, be they criminal or personal, should focus on patterns of behavior and not just points in time. It seems like every day some person is being brought before the court of public opinion because of something they said or did many years ago. To the dismay of the person in the spotlight, every other thing they've ever done is now shoved into the closet while the world focuses on the instance that is counter to legality, morality, or the general ethical standard of the day. My concern is that if we are building a team and we are looking to only add members that have spotless BACKGROUNDS, then we are going to have nobody on our team, including ourselves, because nobody's BACKGROUND is spotless. So since everyone has something in their past that somebody will find offensive, team organizers should look for patterns of behavior that show the person doesn't just have a spot of indiscretion but a line of "bad acting" that permeates their lives.

I'm a huge believer in second (and third…and fourth…) chances because I've been the beneficiary of them. However, that is not necessarily the opinion of many others. The "one mistake" world is alive and well making the issue of BACKGROUND paramount in many ways. Those in charge have to make a determination as to whether a person with a particular BACKGROUND can not only complete the task but also be of benefit to the team. Can we add this person without destroying the team? Please note I said "destroying" the team. Any addition to the team will cause "discomfort" as that's part of the team-building process and cannot be avoided. There are times that the addition of a person might be the "right" thing to do on a personal level, but would completely wreck the team so that it cannot function. It's up to those "getting the big bucks" to determine where adding this BACKGROUND to the BLEND of the team is worth the agitation for the completion of the task and the betterment of the team. And if the leader decides to support such a candidate for inclusion into the organization, the leader has to be willing to stand by not only the decision, but the person, when others disagree.

Before I close I want to throw out a tidbit to those trying to join teams. While it might not be fair (I hate that word, but it's what people say when they don't get their way), your BACKGROUND can hold you back so you need to carefully consider your actions. Employers are checking social media to learn more about the people they are hiring so our personal lives can have a direct negative impact on potential employment and advancement. And because some people subscribe to the "one and done" mentality, doing whatever we are big and bad enough to do can be detrimental. And this isn't just about committing crime. Patterns of behavior that conflict with the direction of the team you want to join may make you incompatible. I can't tell you how many young men and women I had to tell they couldn't join the Air Force because of some indiscretion of their past. It's a shame but it happens more times than it should. Therefore, move forward with your goals in mind understanding that what you do today, could impact your teaming opportunities tomorrow. Let your BACKGROUND be a launching pad to your future instead of a limiting proposition to your success.

No matter what his position or experience in life, there is in everyone more latent than developed ability; far more unused than used power.

-- James Cash Penney

During my career in the Air Force I enjoyed writing annual performance reports. Some folks thought I was sick in the head but I relished the challenge of trying to detail the impact a young officer or Airman had on the unit's mission when limited by the number of lines and the amount of words that could be included on each line. To say that this type of writing was more art than science is an extreme understatement. Not only did we need to know shorter synonyms for the longer words we wanted to use to make sure each phrase fit on one line, we also had to know what words to use and to not use. For example, when I was a young captain, it was generally accepted that the phrase "rock solid" was an indicator that the person in question was just an average guy. In fact, some took it as far to say the phrase implied the person was "as dumb as a rock." So while the person whose report we were writing would celebrate being identified as "rock solid," those "in the know" would carry an opposite view and relegate that person to the lower rungs of the pecking order. Another aspect of the art of writing these reports was the fact that what was a good thing to say in 1998 was classified as a negative indicator in 2005. Despite the regular changes in lexicon, one word that was NEVER supposed to appear on an officer's report was "potential." Because these reports were used by promotion boards, the prevailing opinion of most of the officers I knew was that if an officer had "potential" it meant they weren't doing anything right now. A rock sitting on top of a hill has great "potential" but the fact is that the rock is doing nothing at the moment.

In 2001, I was promoted to the rank of Major. (Yes, I was Major Payne for about six years…unless you ask my wife and she'll tell you I've been Major Payne for about 23 years.) During my promotion ceremony, the mistress of ceremony read the following promotion order:

> The President of the United States, acting upon the recommendation of the Secretary of the Air Force has placed special trust and confidence in the patriotism, integrity, and qualities of Captain Robert Payne, Jr. In view of these special qualities and his demonstrated potential to serve in the higher grade, Captain Payne is promoted to the permanent grade of Major, United States Air Force, 1 May 2001. By special order of the Secretary of the Air Force. (Emphasis added)

Did you see it? Right there in the middle of the order. Despite the disdain for the word "potential" in an annual performance report, the word shows up as one of the key reasons for my promotion, and in fact the promotion of every officer in the United States Air Force. In my words, the Air Force was saying that while they want to hear about an officer's actual performance on the reports, these reports will be used to determine the potential, or LATENCY, of the individual to serve well in the next rank. LATENCY is that ability within a person that is there but hasn't necessarily been actualized and is perhaps the hardest of all of the qualities we are looking for as we build the BLEND of our teams.

As team builders, we can do investigations to determine BACKGROUND and EXPERIENCE and we can conduct personal interviews to ascertain a person's NETWORK and DISPOSITION, but there is not a foolproof method to determine the LATENCY of a person to perform in a new job or environment. Don't believe me? Ask every person that has ever been a personnel director or scout for a professional sports team. They followed the player around for years and interviewed friends, teachers and coaches. They watched miles of game film, gave them tests to determine their mental aptitude, and physicals to make sure their bodies were sound. After all the data was collected and poured over, they decided that this young man was perfect for their team. Unfortunately, more times than not, the LATENCY suggesting this person was destined for greatness at the next level turned out to be, as one of my co-workers used to say, "all sizzle and no steak." They sounded really good but when the time came to perform, there was nothing. And if this just happened in sports, that would be okay but each of us has a story of some person that was anointed the "next big thing" at the job or in the school only to flame out before they got started. Ironically, identifying LATENCY goes the other way too. While many missed the mark on the person they thought would be perfect because that person turned out to be pitiful, there are just as many stories of writing someone off as having no chance to succeed and having them blow up beyond all imagination. Some teachers told Thomas Edison that he was "too stupid to learn anything," 27 publishers rejected Dr. Seuss' first book, and some producer told Oprah Winfrey she was "unfit for TV."

While I am certainly painting a depressing picture of determining the LATENCY in a team member, I have to stress that we must at least make a determination if the person in question fits the part of helping this team move to the next level and complete the assigned tasks. The team builder has to develop a sort of sixth sense about people to see beyond what the data says in order to see LATENCY. However, despite our best attempts to pick the perfect people every time, we are going to miss. We just can't let the misses stop us from making the next attempt. As Mr. Penney said in the quote at the start of this section, "there is in everyone more LATENT than developed ability; far more unused than used power." In the end, I believe the benefits of identifying that LATENCY in a person far outweighs the times we misjudge a person's future ability. Who knows, that person in front of you with the potential to do the job just might have the LATENCY to take your organization higher than it's ever been. You ever hear of that kid from North Carolina who was cut from his high school basketball team as a freshman?

I think his name was Michael. I wonder what ever happened to him...

I usually hire people who have very exemplary work experience. Where they went to school, or what degree they have, really has no play into the hiring decision.

-- Harper Reed

The old philosophical question says, "Which came first, the chicken or the egg?" The conundrum of course is if you say the egg came first, then you have to answer the question of how you get an egg without a chicken to lay it. If you say the chicken came first, then the next apparent question is, "How do you get a chicken without an egg?" While this classic circular argument has been debated for years, I believe there is another question that's just as difficult to answer and much more pressing in the lives of most people. Which came first, the job or the EXPERIENCE? Many a college graduate has left the stage with a shiny new degree in hand and proceeded to their first job interview only to hear, "Tell me about your EXPERIENCE." Running through their mind at that moment is the EXPERIENCE of late night studying, taking tests, and writing papers for the last four to six years. Because that's not the type of EXPERIENCE the hiring agent is looking for, the graduate is denied the job. To make matters worse, the interviewer says, "When you get some EXPERIENCE come back and see us." Now everybody, say the response with me, "HOW DO I GET EXPERIENCE IF NOBODY WILL GIVE ME A JOB?" I know I said that in between my college graduation and coming on active duty and I am 100% convinced that I'm not alone.

While LATENCY tends to be more of a "gut feeling" on the ability of a person to do a job, EXPERIENCE tends to be a more cut and dry determination of a person's actual accomplishment of the task in question. However, we can't be shortsighted in our evaluation of a person's EXPERIENCE because the question, "Has she done this before?" isn't enough to determine if this is the right person for our team. Familiarity with a task is one thing, but familiarity with the method in which our team will accomplish the task is another. Remember our discussion of the NATURE of the task in the previous chapter? I was asked to serve as a calculus tutor which was perfect because I had EXPERIENCE with calculus. However, what I didn't have EXPERIENCE in was doing calculus on a calculator. So, not only did the family need to ask if I had EXPERIENCE with the task of doing calculus, but they really needed to know if I had EXPERIENCE doing the calculus in the way the girls were required to do the calculus.

Actually, there's another piece of EXPERIENCE we have to consider. Yes, we need to know if you have ever done what our team is tasked to do and it is important to know if you've ever done the task in the way our team will do it. But perhaps the best question is, "we're you good at the task?" We assume when someone comes to us with a resume detailing how they've done exactly what we need done, that they accomplished the task in at least a satisfactory manner. This of course is a dangerous assumption. I know people who have EXPERIENCE driving but I'd never put them behind the wheel of my car because they are lousy drivers. Therefore, it is incumbent on the team builder to ascertain not only that a person did the work, but that they did the work well. How do we learn about the quality of the work? The personal interview and talking to not just former employers but coworkers are probably the best ways. Unfortunately, team organizers don't always have to time and resources to conduct thorough checks on the quality of an applicant's work history. In those cases, my recommendation is to do the best you can to make sure you're getting what you want for your team.

For those looking to join teams, overcoming the lack of EXPERIENCE issue will require creativity. In *Three-Dimensional Followership*, I wrote that followers need to know their objective and where they are trying to go when they join the organization. Therefore, if a person is preparing to launch out into the working world, they need to consider where they are trying to go. With the destination in mind, they can begin the process of taking jobs, volunteering for assignments, and sitting with those in that career field, in order to build the EXPERIENCE base necessary to look good on their resume and provide the foundation for a successful interview. Even jobs that don't look like they apply to a future operation can provide the basic skills that a future employer is looking for. To say that you flipped burgers doesn't sound very exciting. However, the job is bigger than just turning meat over because if done right, a person working the grill at a fast food place is monitoring supply and demand and following detailed steps to maximize timely delivery of food and minimize loss of food. Even though it looks like a menial task, those skills apply are necessary in a myriad of jobs around the world.

EXPERIENCE and LATENCY are deeply intertwined and persons with both attributes need to be part of the team. Those with EXPERIENCE offer the team the wisdom of having "been there – done that," while those with LATENCY bring a fresh view to the task and prepare the team to thrive in the future. And even within one person, while their EXPERIENCE might be lacking to some degree, team builders must consider the LATENCY of that person to accomplish the task at hand. Deliberating potential team members on the basis of both these attributes will be time consuming but each moment will be worth the conversation. I might not be able to successfully convince you which comes first, the EXPERIENCE or the job, but I can tell you that we need EXPERIENCED members on our team. However, if they don't have the EXPERIENCE, then we also have to consider their LATENCY and possibly give them the job so they can gain EXPERIENCE.

Networking has been cited as the number one unwritten rule of success in business. Who you know really impacts what you know.

-- Sallie Krawcheck

Back before Donald Trump was the President of the United States, he hosted a show called, 'Celebrity Apprentice." The premise of the show was that a number of "celebrities" (that's in quotes because many of those competing, we knew as kids but hadn't seen in a while) were competing to show their business prowess to Mr. Trump in order to win a prize for the charity of their choice. In season 7, Tiffany Fallon, a Playboy model, was one of the contestants striving to win money for the Walter Reed Society. In the first episode, the two teams were tasked with selling hot dogs in order to see who could raise the most money. While one team made great use of their celebrity status to help sell the hot dogs, Ms. Fallon's team decided to just go with their business sense and raised considerably less money. When it came time for the elimination, Mr. Trump asked Ms. Fallon why she never called her friend, Hugh Hefner, to support the effort. Ms. Fallon's response was that she was saving "Hef" for a worthier task. Unfortunately for her, that task never came as she was "fired" after that first episode. Despite being a celebrity with substantial connections, Ms. Fallon failed her "Apprentice" team and her charity because she failed to capitalize on the NETWORK she brought to the fight.

Growing up I always heard "it's not what you know, it's who you know." That statement is only partially true. More than "who you know," what matters is "who knows you." Because we see stars on TV all the time, we all claim we "know" them. However, there's no benefit to that relationship unless the star in question "knows" us. A NETWORK is the people and organizations an individual can bring to bear in support of the team. And while we want to add people to the team who bring a lot in themselves, team builders should consider what and who else prospective team members can add to the organization to increase the likelihood of success. The interview process is a great mechanism for team organizers to assess the NETWORK of a person. Previous teams, companies, and organizations all serve as potential avenues for partnership and having someone on the current team who can act as a liaison with the other group is vital.

One of the cool things about moving around with my father and in my own Air Force career is the number of people I have met and had the opportunity to interact with. Nearly every time I travel, I am reminded how great it is to have people I know at nearly every stop. What makes those relationships even more valuable is that many of those same people form a NETWORK of people that I can reach out to when a team I am working with needs knowledge, talent, resources, or abilities that isn't resident on my current team at the time. Rather than cold-calling an unknown commodity, it is much better to have someone on the team who "knows somebody" that can support the team on part of a task. Therefore, a team member's EXPERIENCE extends beyond just the things they know but also the people they can reach out and touch when the team is in need. In this day of outsourcing, this method of receiving assistance from persons or organizations not necessarily part of the team makes the sum much greater than the individual parts.

Even as I type this I can hear someone thinking, "You're telling me to use people for who they know." And to that complaint, I have to say, "You're right." If we are building a team to be successful, we are already planning on using a person's intellect, EXPERIENCE, gifts, talents, ideas, and abilities so why wouldn't we use their NETWORK as well? There's a Christian gospel song that says "99 ½ won't do." Well when it comes to bringing the most to the team, using only part of what a person brings to the table won't do either. If everything a team member has isn't accessible to the team, including their NETWORK, then the team's opportunities for success are diminished. It happened to Tiffany Fallon's team on "Celebrity Apprentice" and it could be happening to your team now.

I am determined to be cheerful and happy in whatever situation I may find myself. For I have learned that the greater part of our misery or unhappiness is determined not by our circumstance but by our disposition.

-- Martha Washington

My daughter loves to do puzzles. When we buy puzzles for her, all the pieces of the puzzle are in the box. (At least they start that way. Somehow after she gets the puzzle, there seems to be fewer than the required number of pieces.) At the time of purchase, the pieces are together in one place. They exist in the same space. They are together…and unfortunately together is a problem. Together is a problem because the puzzle isn't fulfilling its designed purpose by just being together. The pieces of the puzzle only fulfill their purpose when they are united. What's the difference between being "together" and being "united?" "Together" means they are occupying a similar space but "united" means they are interacting with each other in order to accomplish a higher purpose. I think you see where I'm going with this. There are a lot teams, organizations, and groups that are together, but they are not united. (Can I get an amen?!?!) Those teams are occupying the same space, wearing the same uniforms, and supposedly working the same tasks, but they are not interacting in such a way to achieve the created purpose of the organization. The biggest issue in blocking the unity of the team isn't the individual BACKGROUNDS, LATENCY, EXPERIENCE, or NETWORKS, but the DISPOSITION of the team members. The DISPOSITION of a person, as defined by dictionary.com, is "the predominant or prevailing tendency of one's spirit; natural mental and emotional outlook or mood; characteristic attitude"[2] and if the DISPOSITIONS of teammates don't mesh, the team will never succeed.

Of all the factors in successfully putting together the proper BLEND of the team, perhaps the most damaging to the success of the team is bad DISPOSITIONS among the team members. We spend a lot of time talking about "toxic leadership" but I really think we should probably spend more time discussing "toxic followership" and "toxic team members" because team members with poor DISPOSITIONS can infect the morale of the team faster than anything else. It's one thing for people to attack the team from the outside, but when the attacks come from the inside, it's a whole different thing.

Anytime we put more than two people together, we have to consider how they will interact with one another. Those of us with siblings know that even if people come from the same parents, are raised by the same rules, and live in the same environment, that personalities and attitudes can be vastly different and those differences are the basis for many disagreements. Team builders have to take into account the DISPOSITIONS of those being added to the team to ensure

---

[2] https://www.dictionary.com/browse/disposition?s=t, accessed 30 August 2019.

they are prepared for any disagreements that may occur. Unfortunately for many leaders, this "softer" side of leadership isn't any fun so we just tell those on the team to "get along and make it work." However, just like in our homes with our kids, that order falls on deaf ears and though the task may get done, the team is steadily unraveling from the inside. Similar to EXPERIENCE, understanding DISPOSITION goes beyond what's printed on the resume. Team builders have to go deeper than the piece of paper and do due diligence in order to determine whether or not the person being added to the team will mesh well with the team.

Interestingly enough, there may be times when a team organizer purposely seeks someone with a DISPOSITION which is counter to those that currently reside on the team. For instance, if the team has grown stagnant and lethargic, someone with an aggressive, forceful DISPOSITION might be needed to spur the team in new direction. Similarly, a team filled with detail-oriented analytical minds could benefit from a long-range free-thinker. Remember, this is about finding the proper BLEND for the team, and just like the pieces of a puzzle, every piece is shaped differently, but every piece is required to build the picture we are looking for. If we ignore the DISPOSITION of the team members, we might as well just put the team together and leave because they will never be united.

Taking a 3-D Look at Your Team

1. What role does diversity of BACKGROUND have on your team?

2. What mechanism does your team employ to identify LATENCY in team members?

3. What EXPERIENCE does your team need to improve performance?

4. Who on your team has a NETWORK that can move your team forward in accomplish its goals?

5. What DISPOSITION on your team is detrimental to team success? What's being done to mitigate that DISPOSITION?

Chapter 4: Build the Team to TEND to Themselves

Fresh out of college, you tend to join a company because it's a job. But, you tend to stay because it becomes a career; you start to feel at home. In the beginning of your career, you're focused on you: 'I like this place because I'm doing rewarding work; they take good care of me; the people are nice; there's runway for me,' etc.

-- Ursula Burns

While John 3:16 is probably the most famous verse in all the bible, the most famous set of verses has to be Psalm 23. Even for those who haven't spent any time in Sunday School, the first few verses probably ring a bell:

> [1]The Lord is my shepherd; I shall not want.
> [2]He makes me to lie down in green pastures; He leads me beside the still waters.
> [3]He restores my soul; He leads me in the paths of righteousness for His name's sake.

This Psalm, composed by the shepherd-turned-king, David, delivers the quintessential picture of God's loving care for His people. As a good shepherd, God understands the nature of his sheep and provides for them. The Psalm illustrates God's supplying to the needs of the sheep so there is no want in them, leading them to places of comfortable rest, and attending to their emotional needs while guiding them in the right direction. It is the responsibility of a shepherd and the loving function of the God of the bible, to TEND to his sheep because the shepherd knows that he cannot expect quality wool or meat if the needs of the sheep are left unfulfilled. Similarly, a team builder must ensure the team has instruments in place to TEND to the team if he or she expects the team to be productive.

I began to understand the importance of the TEND of the team when I was a recruiter. Early in my career I spent my time trying to convince young men and women to join the Air Force. I quickly learned that recruiting success required taking different tracks with each member of the family. The student usually wanted to know what job they'd be doing. They focused their questions on the excitement of flying planes or serving as a nurse. Fathers were often more concerned with paying for school. They were asking me to "show them the money." Mothers, on the other hand, wanted to know how Air Force ROTC in the near term, and the Air Force in the long term, would take care of "their baby." They would ask questions about the safety, healthcare, housing, family life, and post-service opportunities. Since in many families, what momma said was law, I needed to have my best answers for her. If I couldn't clearly and completely explain to mom how the Air Force would TEND to her child, the chance of that student joining ROTC and pursuing an Air Force career was almost nil. Since those days, I have tried to pay closer attention to how the teams I was a part of looked after the members of the team. In *Three-Dimensional Leadership*, I mentioned the oft-quoted adage that "people don't care how much you know until they know how much you care." Well, the way a team shows they care for those on the team is by TENDING to their needs.

To "TEND," according to dictionary.com, is to "to look after; watch over and care for; minister to or wait on with service"[3] and how the team TENDS to itself is the linchpin to continuity and lasting success of the organization. The TEND of the team is the team organizer's attempt to answer the "what's in it for me?" question that potential team members often ask when considering whether or not to join. The TEND of the team is also what sets one organization apart from other similar organizations. For our purposes, the TEND is the **T**raining, **E**ncouragement, **N**otice, and **D**evelopment the organization offers to those who are part of the team. Yes, we want to add the people necessary to reach the END of the task and to enhance the BLEND of the team, but if the TEND isn't right, the longevity of the team is in question as team members find new shepherds, run to greener pastures, and seek quieter waters.

The best training program in the world is absolutely worthless without the will to execute it properly, consistently, and with intensity.

-- John Romaniello

For a period of time while I was stationed at Malmstrom Air Force Base in Great Falls, MT, I served as an evaluator. In that duty I was responsible for conducting evaluations on

---

[3] https://www.dictionary.com/browse/tend#, accessed 10 September 2019

missile combat crew members to determine if they were ready to be certified in their positions or if they could keep their certifications. This was truly one of the more thankless jobs I ever had because the evaluators were always the bad guy. When someone made a mistake, we had to document the error and then tell the crew members about their error during the out brief. Needless to say, nobody ever liked hearing about the things they did wrong during an evaluation so there always seemed to be a lot of tension between the crew and the evaluators. Periodically, we would tell someone about a deviation they made from standard operating procedures and the person would quickly respond, "That's not how I was TRAINED." They rationalized that because they hadn't received the requisite TRAINING, that any mistake was not their fault and should be immediately excused. This back and forth over TRAINING was very frustrating because while our unit had a standardized TRAINING program so that every officer would receive the exact same TRAINING, differences in the ability, desire, and consistency of the individual instructors allowed for some doubt as to whether or not the officers in question were TRAINED properly. While we could say they were supposed to be TRAINED that way, we couldn't guarantee the TRAINING occurred.

I'd love to say that the adequacy of TRAINING was only a problem at the one assignment in my Air Force career. Unfortunately, this issue has reared its ugly head at every stop I made throughout my 24-year military career and extended into my time in ministry and civilian work. Again, maybe it's just me and the places I've worked, but TRAINING seems to be a problem for organizations of all types and in all places. The fact is that I see the problem getting worse and worse because our expectations of people are so high. We simply expect everyone to "just know" how to do the things we need done and we get very upset when they don't. For example, one of the requirements in nearly every job posting is the ability to operate the Microsoft Suite. Simple enough right? There aren't too many of us who haven't typed a letter in Word or built a spreadsheet in Excel. But if we think back to our discussion of the NATURE of the task, just because a person knows how to type a letter in Word doesn't mean they know how to create the type of document the team needs completed. So during the interview, the person boldly answers "yes" to the question about familiarity with Word, but on the first day of the job, everything crumbles because she can't mail merge documents. Because the team figured all new employees would just know how to complete the task and everyone is too busy to help the new person, they don't have a plan to TRAIN her on the finer details of the task. She will just have to "figure it out on her own." After all, that's the way the majority of the team learned so she might as well learn that way too. Do you see the insanity of this? The END of the team is in jeopardy and the BLEND of the team is damaged because there was no TRAINING for new employees.

I can almost see you nodding your head as you think back to the job you had and the frustration you felt because while you were motivated to do the job, you never received the TRAINING so you eventually left the job...or worse yet, you stayed in the job and performed way below your ability because you figured if they don't care to give you TRAINING, you're not going to care to do the work. From our negative experiences, we should all clearly see that a comprehensive and consistent TRAINING program is vital to the success of the team. Whether the team chooses formal classroom TRAINING, on-the-job TRAINING, shadow TRAINING, or a combination of these doesn't matter. What matters is that employees are given the TRAINING to perform at the peak for their ability. Oh and by the way, training isn't just for the guy who shows up on day one. As times change, there should be continual and refresher TRAINING processes to make sure employees maintain their sharpness. In fact, let me close this section with a story that has a number of versions but this one is my favorite:

> Two woodcutters were competing against each other as to who could chop down the most trees in a day. Both started hacking away within earshot of each other. After an hour, Sam stopped. Fred was puzzled but carried on chopping. Five minutes later, he could again hear the swing of Sam's axe. Another hour went by, and Sam again seemed to stop chopping for a few minutes. Fred was thrilled. He became more confident that he would win. So he kept chopping away, pausing now and again to wipe away the perspiration from his forehead. Sam's "start and

stop" continued for the rest of the day, and Fred's delight grew. At the end of the day, however, Fred was surprised to discover that Sam had felled more trees. "How can this be? I never stopped chopping once but you kept taking a break!" "Yes, but I stopped to sharpen my axe," Sam replied.

If team builders and leaders don't have a plan to "sharpen the axe" of the team members through a strong TRAINING program, there will be a lot of activity but very little achievement. …and then you will have to deal with team members making mistakes and doing inferior work just to let you know that they were never TRAINED to do better.

Employees are a company's greatest asset - they're your competitive advantage. You want to attract and retain the best; provide them with encouragement, stimulus, and make them feel that they are an integral part of the company's mission.

-- Anne M. Mulcahy

When I started playing organized football, one of the very first things our coaches did was to teach us how to huddle. It seemed sort of silly because I wanted to run and catch and tackle and this time spent standing around talking to each other was a waste of time. Like most things in my life, I eventually realized the wisdom of their approach because they were imparting on us not just a lesson for football, but a lesson for life. That lesson was that the huddle was important. Yes, running, blocking and throwing are extremely important but without the huddle, how would we know where to run, who to block, and who to throw to? The huddle was the place where you received your orders. During the games I realized there were added benefits to the huddle. You see, when we made a good play, we could go back to the huddle and have people high five us and tell us how good we did. It was a place of congratulations. But since we didn't always do well, the huddle also served as a place of consolation. We could go back to the huddle and have the team remind us that we still mattered and were still necessary. Both the congratulations and the consolation found in the huddle formed the ENCOURAGEMENT the team offered to every team member. If you think ENCOURAGEMENT is important to a bunch of 10-year olds on a football field, you should see the difference ENCOURAGEMENT makes on the teams you find yourself on.

If statistics are to be believed, we live in a very discouraged world. Depression and suicide are way up as many people have decided that their lives are hopeless and they themselves are useless. It's one thing for this attitude to permeate a guest on Steve Harvey's talk show but it's another thing for it to occur in the halls and cubicles of our workspaces. For a team builder to take the position that "as long as the people are doing their job, I don't care how they feel" is for the team builder to set the team up for eventual failure. Like TRAINING, organizations need intentional means to provide ENCOURAGEMENT to the team members if for no other reason to remind them that the team sees them as individuals and not just a piece of machinery that can be easily replaced. Perhaps this is a great place for TRAINING to come in because senior management may have to ensure middle managers are TRAINED to not only maintain the company's bottom line but also manage the company's best assets which are the people. Please note that this is not about being warm and fuzzy and offering daily hugs as people come into work (although there are certainly days I could use that). This is about recognizing that people have feelings and they like a pat on the back once in a while. And remember that pats on the back go both ways. As a pastor, I've given people pats on the back for graduating from high school on the same day as I had to pat others on the back to console them for getting into legal trouble. The point is that the pat on the back is a method of letting someone know that the team sees them and what they are going through, be it positive or negative.

A huge responsibility for team builders is not just finding the right people to be on the team but also establishing the culture of that team. For best results, may I suggest a culture of ENCOURAGEMENT? A place where not just supervisors, but co-workers and peers regularly seek opportunities to celebrate one another in times of success and lift each other up in times of defeat and discouragement. If you've read my previous two books in this series, you are probably having a flashback moment right now. In *Three-Dimensional Leadership*, I asserted that leaders must

AFFIRM those that follow them. Similarly, in *Three Dimensional Followership*, I stated that followers have the responsibility to ENCOURAGE their fellow followers. This repeat of concepts isn't because I couldn't think of any other words to fit in my acrostics. This is extremely intentional because ENCOURAGEMENT is a responsibility of every member of the team, leaders and followers alike, and must be made an inherent part of the organization's culture. Think about the difference between going to work in a place where everyone is backbiting and fussing versus going to work in a place where you understand everyone in the group has got your back, when you're on top of your game and when you seem to be striking out at every at bat. The culture of ENCOURAGEMENT would not only make you want to come to work, but to give the best in you for the success of the team. We don't have a lot of time in the huddle but we'd be wise to take part of that time to provide the ENCOURAGEMENT, the consolation and congratulations our team needs so everyone can focus on the marching orders for the moment. Ready…Break!!!

Research indicates that employees have three prime needs: Interesting work, recognition for doing a good job, and being let in on things that are going on in the company.

-- Zig Ziglar

In 2018 the University of Miami started a tradition with their football team called "the turnover chain." While it is debatable whether or not the Hurricanes were first college program to celebrate turnovers in this fashion, there is no question that the school took the practice to a whole new level. If you haven't seen Miami play over the last couple of years, then you haven't seen this spectacle and it is a sight to see. Whenever a Miami defensive player recovers a fumble or makes an interception they dash to the sidelines where a 6.5 pound, 10-karat piece of jewelry is placed around their neck and they get to preen for the cameras. While it might seem silly to the average fan, and aggravating to opponents, I don't believe it's coincidental that Miami has been one of the nation's leaders in forcing turnovers since the advent of the turnover chain. While you'd think playing the game they love on national TV would be enough, these young men are excited and energized by the NOTICE they receive for making a game-changing play. A team built for success will ensure team members receive recognition for positive contributions to the team.

Similar to the creation of a culture of ENCOURAGEMENT, a program focused on NOTICE may take extra effort for team builders because we often mirror-image our personality on others and if we don't need ENCOURAGEMENT or NOTICE, then we assume others around us don't need them either. And while many people are perfectly fine with a silent thumbs up, others are driven by public awards that highlight them for the work they've done. One of my favorite quotes is one I learned during my military history classes in college where Napoleon says, "*A soldier will fight long and hard for a bit of colored ribbon.*" The great general was making the case that the prospect of reward allowing an individual to stand apart from the team was a driving factor to improved performance. Also notice from Napoleon's quote that the "carrot" in this case is tangible. That "bit of colored ribbon" provides a visual reminder to the individual and the entire team that this person stood out in their duties.

Many of the organizations I have been a part of have awards programs where the company intentionally sets out to NOTICE team members for exceptional performance. I need to foot stomp those last two words, "exceptional performance," because we are rapidly becoming a culture that gives everyone a reward for simply existing. I heard the argument when I was in Little League when the parents didn't want to give a Most Valuable Player trophy to Vic because that would make the other kids feel bad. Heck, all of us kids knew Vic was the best player on the team so I'm not sure how anyone would have been upset by them awarding the obvious. That interaction has affected me throughout the years because I see our refusal to provide NOTICE to those who deserve the attention as deflating to their desire to continue to perform at a high level. Maybe I'm guilty of mirror-imaging myself here, but I remember how it felt to truly be an exceptional team member and receive the same general accolades as the rest of the team. Although I never stopped giving my all because that's my personality, I can't deny the thought crossed my mind to move on from that team to a place where I could be appreciated. If they aren't going to NOTICE my extra effort, why give it? Not sure I should admit this to you or not but this attitude has bled into my marriage. I have made it abundantly clear to my wife that if I clean out the garage, she better recognize my efforts or I will never clean out the garage again. Yes, I did the work because the work needed to be done but even more so, I did the work so she'd NOTICE. I'm not saying this is entirely healthy but I firmly believe that if there is a plan to NOTICE the efforts of individuals with tangible rewards, their desire to perform at a high level will increase. I could be wrong about this but given the number of players at the University of Miami trying to make game-changing plays in order to put that chain around their neck, I have the feeling that NOTICE matters.

There was a moment when I was watching Martin Lawrence and Will Smith in 'Bad Boys' that I felt, you know, inspired. I don't know if I was proud, because so many people do the work. Everyone's part of a team that develops over the years and gives people chances. There have been some good moments watching people develop.
-- Russell Simmons

I know this is going to sound old fashioned but I love board games. Monopoly, Life, Sorry, and the like are what I grew up on. However, the simple classics of chess and checkers are probably my all-time favorites. It's interesting that the games are played on the same kind of board and have pieces that have assigned ways of moving. In fact, they are interesting team building exercises in and of themselves because part of the challenge is keeping the enough of the right pieces over the course of the game in order to win. One aspect of each game that is more noticeable in checkers than in chess is the ability for the pieces to improve themselves, or DEVELOP. The major strategy of most checkers players is getting pieces to the other side of the board so they can be kinged. Being kinged allows the piece to move in directions it was unable to move in before. This principle is also a part of chess but less often seen. Pawns are the weakest pieces on the board, only able to move straight ahead one space at a time unless they are moving one space diagonally to take another piece. (Yes, I know they can move forward two spaces on their first move. I'm not trying to cheat anyone.) While the pawn is the weakest piece on the board, it enjoys a unique DEVELOPMENT opportunity. If a pawn can reach the back row on the opposite side of the board, that pawn can be "DEVELOP" into any other chess piece. Therefore, what was a weak pawn has the potential to turn into an all-powerful queen by simply moving forward. (That'll preach right there.) Hopefully you can see the point. Quite often people join teams and start at the bottom and get very frustrated because all they can see is being on the bottom. They are a pawn and the only hope before them is being a pawn. Team builders have to have plans in place to ensure persons joining the team have DEVELOPMENT opportunities so they can move up from where they started to what they hope to be.

Too often I believe team builders and leaders simply expect DEVELOPMENT to happen. They don't have any plans to DEVELOP the personnel figuring that when the "higher ups" leave, we'll just fill in with the next person. Unfortunately, because we often don't necessarily know when that person is leaving, we are taken by surprise and the next person in line for the position isn't ready to fully assume the role. DEVELOPMENT must be an intentional process to prepare entry level team members for positions of greater responsibility. It is in the DEVELOPMENT plan for the team that the team builds on and hones the LATENCY that we considered when we hired the person. Many of us know the frustration of being hired on promises of swift advancement only to wallow in the same position year after year only to be told that "your time is coming." I personally can handle that my time is coming but when I'm not given a chance to at least take a step in that direction periodically, I start to consider other opportunities.

Perhaps my favorite example of this was my first job at Hardee's. When I applied for the job, I wanted to be a cashier because I wasn't about cooking for anyone. However, when they hired me, they handed me a brown, polyester uniform and a spatula and told me to get over to the grill. I hated it. It was hot and at the end of the day I smelled like grease. Not that I had much game with the ladies back then anyways, but I definitely had no game smelling like a double burger and a side of fries. Over and over again I asked the leadership what could I do to move off the grill and get a "promotion" to the front line and over and over again they ignored my pleas. At that point I considered quitting because I didn't want to be a part of a team that wanted to sequester me away in a dead-end job. Before I decided to quit though, I talked to one of the young ladies who worked the cash register and asked her to show me how to cashier. Because it was Hardee's, we were often very slow so during those slow times, I would go up front, take a person's order and then run to the back and fix the food. I'm not sure what management was doing during these "DEVELOPMENT" sessions, but it placated me somewhat that I could at least do something beyond flip burgers and drop fries. Then one day my big break came. A couple of cashiers called in sick and the manager couldn't find anyone to come in. At that point, one of the young ladies that showed me how to take orders spoke up and said, "Bobby can work the front. We've trained him." Management was skeptical but she insisted and after taking some orders under supervision, I was allowed to solo. From then on, I was a cashier. Since my Hardee's days, I have made it my purpose to help people see the path to increased responsibility if that was their desire. What that meant for me in each environment was that I had to have a plan to DEVELOP them before I sat down to talk with them. Because Hardee's didn't have a DEVELOPMENT plan, they risked losing an employee who had aspirations of more than food preparation.

The biblical adage of "He who is faithful in little will be given much" (Luke 16:10) is a key part to the process because the team member has an important role in their DEVELOPMENT. Unfortunately, too many employees are so focused on the DEVELOPMENT to the next job that they never perform the current job in a satisfactory manner. Therefore, team leaders need to clearly identify the path to promotion and greater responsibility, but also ensure the team members understand their performance matters if they are going to DEVELOP. While the path of a checker's piece seems boring and is filled with challenges and opposition, if the piece follows the prescribed course to DEVELOPMENT, they will be able to say in the immortal words of Rudy Huxtable from the Cosby Show, "*King Me! King Me!*"

Taking a 3-D Look at Yourself

1. What TRAINING do members on your team need to be better at their jobs?

2. How do you and individual team members ENCOURAGE one another?

3. What programs are in place for individuals to receive NOTICE for a job well-done?

4. Where are the opportunities on your team for individuals to DEVELOP?

Chapter 5: So Now What?

In the biblical book of Genesis, after creating the world and saying that everything He had made was good, God finally identifies one thing that isn't good. He says in Genesis 2:18, "It is not good for man to be alone." We traditionally apply this verse to marriage and while it certainly applies there, throughout the bible we see God applying that verse to human relationships in general. In my limited mind, this verse is where God indicates the desperate need for human beings to team up and work together. That we need teams is obvious. The more pressing issue is process we use to build or decide to join those teams we need. Whether we are looking for one other person to spend the rest of our lives with or a group of people to provide goods and services to the world, **how** we put the team together matters and serious questions must be answered if the team is going to be succeed.

A team is built to succeed when the team builder and those joining the team understand the END of the team. All parties need to have a firm understanding of the EFFORT, NATURE, and DURATION required to satisfy the task. The biggest problem with America's effort during the Vietnam Conflict is that nobody knew what the END was. Because there was no clear objective to the task, the team that was drafted and formed was doomed to failure. Many of our teams have mimicked this and there shouldn't be any surprise that the results were less than satisfactory

A team is built to succeed when the team builder and those joining the team understand the BLEND of the team. The art of team building is like cooking…finding and mixing the right ingredients ensures the flavor will be satisfying to all who interact with the team. The BACKGROUND, LATENCY, EXPERIENCE, NETWORK, and DISPOSITION of the team members need to be carefully managed to make sure that a team that understands and meets the END of the task doesn't destroy itself in the process. We are looking for "one team, one fight" rather than "one team always fighting."

A team is built to succeed when the team builder and those joining the team understand the TEND of the team. I said it before and I'll say it again, "Nobody cares how much you know until they know how much you care." Well, this is certainly a leadership principle that every leader should observe and those putting teams together should make sure programs and processes are in place to demonstrate care of the team members by providing TRAINING, ENCOURAGEMENT, NOTICE, and DEVELOPMENT. Turnover on teams, especially enduring teams, is inevitable but members will be less likely to want to leave teams that see them as more than just pieces to be used and treat them as individuals in need of support and growth opportunities.

If you haven't guessed it, I'm a team guy. While I love being alone, I prefer to operate in teams. I love celebrating victory with others and also having someone to console me when defeat rears its ugly head. I've been on great teams that didn't last and I've been on lousy teams that lasted too long. I've been the team captain on the playground and I've been the guy just hoping to be picked to work on the project. Through every experience, I've come to understand that we have to do this team thing better if we are going to truly be successful. Success cannot be limited to just the task because the team as a whole and each individual matters. Success cannot be just measured in terms of the team because the team is made up of individuals and that team of individuals must complete a task. Success cannot be just measured by the happiness of the individual because the individuals must contribute to the health of the team and the conclusion of the task. Team success requires a three-dimensional approach where team builders and joiners are committed to success in every area. We have to build better teams. We have to join better teams. But better will not just happen. It's going to take EFFORT. This concerted EFFORT to address the task, the team and the individuals will take a lot of work but it is work that will be worth it. So my friend, you are on the clock. You need to make a choice. Will you build or join a team designed for three-dimensional success or will you do it your own way and try to go alone? While you are debating that decision, God already casted His vote. He says going alone is "not good." Just saying.